THE SLAIN BIRDS

By the same author:

The Slain Birds
Michael Longley

WAKE FOREST UNIVERSITY PRESS

First North American edition

Copyright © Michael Longley, 2022

All rights reserved. No part of this book may
be reproduced in any form without prior
permission in writing from the publishers.

For permission, write to:
Wake Forest University Press
Post Office Box 7333
Winston-Salem, NC 27109
wfupress.wfu.edu
wfupress@wfu.edu

ISBN 978-1-930630-99-4 (paperback)
LCCN 2021945779

Designed and typeset by Peter Barnfather

Publication of this book was generously
supported by the Boyle Family Fund.

for my grandchildren
Amelia, Ben, Conor, Eddie, Jacob, Katie, Maisie

A blackbird begins it at the window,
Then high above the townland skylarks
Out of sight, then on the periphery
Unmelodious choughs and ravens, then
A curlew anticipating evening:
The dawn chorus at all my locations.

for the sake of the souls of the slain birds sailing
DYLAN THOMAS

Tawny Owl

At least the motorist who stunned the owl
Stopped and lifted the body onto the verge
And there Amelia and Maisie found it.
A friend will soak the wings in salty water
To make shaman-fans for smudging rites,
Another wants the skull for her collection
And will have to bury it for one whole year.
(Why are there no tawny owls in Ireland?
Do you know that Eric Hosking photograph
Of the tawny that robbed him of an eye,
Rage and terror cramped between the branches?)
Maisie sketches in charcoal its underside,
Amelia hugs to herself all the feathers:
'I will look after you, poor owl,' she sighs.

Ritual

for Dunia Shakti

With rosemary and rosemary-ash and sage
You buried the owl near your rowan tree.
You used a black obsidian stone as well,
The one the pendulum chose, and water.

You thanked the tawny owl for coming here
And the grandmothers and grandfathers
Of the four directions, above and below.
After this shocking death you sang a song.

Eyelid

Amelia opens the tawny owl's eyelid
And finds a concentration of the night.

Drawing

Teach me how to draw, Sarah,
Eye to hand—a heat-shimmer
Of approximations—a face
Coming clear—an otter, a hare,
A self-portrait, me even.

Artistic daughter, you
Give birth to my old age.
Your charcoal fills with colours.
You leave a space unmarked
And create a swan.

Amelia's Model

I

In her model of the solar system
My seven-year-old cosmologist
Ties to a barbeque skewer
With fuse wire the planets, buttons:
For Venus an ivory button,
Mercury silver beside the sun,
Mother-of-pearl for Jupiter,
Red and green for Mars and Earth,
For Saturn's rings a pipe-cleaner,
So that in the outer darkness
Close to the kitchen her brown eyes
Represent Uranus, Neptune.

II

Amelia, you didn't include Pluto
In your wire sculpture of the solar system:
Tiny and very far away, an ice
World of ice mountains and methane snow,
A dance of five moons unlit by the sun,
The god of the afterlife's kingdom—
We shall go there when we die, dear child.

Merlin

Is that a peregrine or kestrel
Quartering the townland?
We sit above Corragaun
And the dwindling lake and look
Towards Templedoomore
And the lost burial mound.
Are we waiting to die, my love?
What's happening behind us?
Have our snowy heads been seen
By the merlin we cannot see?

Isolation

Old age and the virus
Keep me from driving west
To join sanderlings
Along the shore-line,
Oyster-catchers beyond,
Whoopers on the lake,
Tufted ducks and coots
And the heron waiting,
Acrobatic choughs
And talkative ravens,
Otters effervescent
Between trout and elver,
Stoat and hare sharing
Our rock of the wall-fern.

Sneezewort

Now that the virus keeps us apart
I try to remember exactly where
I introduced my first grandson
Years ago to this unassuming
Supposed cure for cough and cold,
And he drew a picture of it
Above spindly letters, sneezewort,
Petals arranged like a daisy's
Around a grey-and-yellow eye
That might irradiate sickness:
Was it where a runnel murmurs
Into the lake without a name?

Plovers

I

An anonymous Tommy
On the first day of the Somme
Guarded for half an hour,
For an eternity,
A plover's nest, to protect
The eggs from being trampled,
The rainbird's eggs.

II

Under heavy fire the plover that pretends
A broken wing dies of a broken wing.

Dartford Warbler

It arrived in the post
In answer to my poems,
Jeff's sparky portrait
Of this rarest bird,
A Dartford warbler
Among gorse blossom,
Once only in my life
Glimpsed in Picardy
Where the Downs continue,
When I stood at the poet's
Grave and asked myself
Had Edward seen it too.

Dear Mother

after Private Herbert Beattie: a found poem

Just to let you know i am safe and thank God for it
for we had a ruf time of it in the charge we made
don't let on to V Quinn mother or Archers mother
they must be killed wounded for they are missen
of roll call and tell Hugh the fellow that youst
to run along with E Ferguson called Eddie Mallin
he youst to have Pigens if Hugh dus not no him
McKeown nows him tell them he was killed tell them
ther is not another grosvenor Rd fellow left but myself
Mother wee were tramping over the dead i think
there is onely about 4 hundred left out of about 13
hundred Mother if god spers me to get home safe
i wil have something uful to tell you if hell
is any wores i would not like to go to it Mother
let me here from you soone as you can this is all
i can say at present your loving son Herbie
show my Father this letter and tell him to writ

Quatrains

I

What did they talk about on picnic trips,
The concentration camp's senior staff?
To whom did they post their happy photos,
'Lots of love from all of us at Auschwitz'?

II

They put up a Christmas tree in Auschwitz
And stacked as presents underneath the tree
Bodies of prisoners who had died that day.
Then the assembled ranks sang 'Silent Night'.

III

The deadly smoke belching night and day
And screams from the tortured and dying
Meant that birds stopped singing at Auschwitz.
Sanity was remembering their names.

Ravine

In a quiet Polish ravine
Two German soldiers with rifles
Can murder so many women.
Oh, their ageing breasts look sore.
Keep your blouses on, my dear ones.

Bullets are saved for slaughtering grown-ups
And are not wasted on little children
Who suffocate underneath their families
And drown in their parents' blood and urine.

Onlooker

On their way home, near the railway station
Onlookers gather round the massacre
As a citizen with a heavy pole
Clubs one Jew after another to death.
A small boy sits on his father's shoulders
For a better view of what is happening.

Lullaby

When a ghetto baby dies
the mother sings a lullaby
lullay my child lullay lullay
her breasts are weeping milk
lullay my child lullay lullay

Maps of Gloucestershire

after Helen Thomas: a found poem

Ivor Gurney at once spread them out on his bed
And he and I spent the whole time I was there
Tracing with our fingers the lanes and byways
And villages of which he knew every step
And over which Edward had also walked.
He spent that hour in re-visiting his home,
In spotting a village or a track, a hill or a wood
And seeing it all in his mind's eye, with flowers
And trees, stiles and hedges, a mental vision
Sharper and more actual for his heightened
Intensity. He trod, in a way we who were sane
Could not emulate, the lanes and fields he knew
And loved so well, his guide being his finger
Tracing the way on the map. It was most deeply
Moving, and I knew that I had hit on an idea
That gave him more pleasure than anything else
I could have thought of. For he had Edward
As companion in this strange perambulation...

Heatwave

Feet on fire, a bath filled with cold water,
I sit on the edge to cool my ankles
And insomnia, and in the small hours
I read Ivor Gurney, and I understand
His obscurity and muddle, poems
That know more than he knows, more than I know:
A Severnside hedge-pool's cloud-reflections,
Face-dissolving blood-ponds of Passchendaele.
He washes my feet the way Jesus would.

Home

Carrigskeewaun is David Cabot's home:
I have learned all about spring tides from him,
Stiles and stepping stones, when whoopers arrive
And leave, snow buntings at Allaran Point,
Dooaghtry's technicolour snails, and marsh
Marigolds (Penny's flowers): a state of mind,
Otter-sightings, elvers, leverets, poetry,
The Owenadornaun's five syllables.

Names

I twine our souls with names from this landscape
As the neap tide uncovers Carricknashinnagh
Close to where we swim; the way to Tonakeera
Where we walk as to the islands; Barnabaun
And Kinnakillew—nearly off the map—
Drifts of melody—and Trawleckachoolia
Where we shall dander until the day we die.

Gaslight

Do you remember those early gas-mantle days,
Powdery nets for capturing light and silence;
When the outboard motor spluttered in its shed
And the water failed, buckets carried from the lake
Through yellow flags; sooty fireside implements,
The crane we never used; newspapers at the hearth
For hailstones; rags soaked in methylated spirits
To start the pilot light and inspire the fridge?
I shall lie cheek to cheek with chilly tiles for hours.
I shall trundle two gas cylinders into place.

Electricity

When the electrification of Carrigskeewaun
Brought poles marching from Claggan and Kinnakillew
Across 'the last remaining unspoiled vista'
(Rosemary Garvey's words), I mourned the death of gaslight,
But oh, how the electric blanket warmed my soul!

———

Godwit

I am filming with David Cabot
And Michael Viney—on location
In our soul-landscape—a windy day—
A sudden bird—a snipe I suggest—
A godwit—Michael corrects me—
From our ornithologist—silence—
So Michael pins it down—a feather
In his cap—a bar-tailed godwit.

Skylarks

At Carrigskeewaun
Skylarks are sky-
Climbing, soul-dots
At the apex, wind's
Vocal chords and
Our own outpouring.

Cuckoo

The one cuckoo at Carrigskeewaun
Calling from alders across the lake
Leaves behind, after a single day,
Solitariness, silence, mute swans.

Path

Through the obstreperous galvanised gate
And over the brown trout's little bridge
I have carried children on my shoulders,
Hockerty-cockerty, then grandchildren.

Nests

When I die I want you to close my eyes
And look into the soul-space for ever
As once you looked into the skylark's nest
Snug beside the well at Carrigskeewaun
Or, from below, the swallows' home precarious
In the cottage porch and your quietude,
Or the mallard's nest at watery Claggan
Deep among yellow flags beneath the sky
And your concentration counting the eggs.

Foam

And now, in my old age, I remember
That we made love in the Thallabaun dunes
Not too far away from the badgers' sett,
And then swam naked at Allaran Point
Stepping over otter prints, preserving
Signs of life, sea-foam between our toes.

Winter Solstice

I

Christmas Eve: you turn eighty today, love,
Separated by the virus from children
And grandchildren, my elderly bride asleep
Beside me at the winter solstice, days
Growing longer, the family returning,
At the bedroom window budding catkins,
House sparrows in the pink-flowered hawthorn.

II

Now David reports from Carrigskeewaun
Choughs calling above the cottage—*pshaw pshaw*—
On their way to the Claggan roosting-cliff;
And sets free in my imagination
The swans you counted in your nightdress once
Long ago at dawn when we were lovers—
Twenty whoopers fading into snowlight.

Moon

You dreamed that you had landed on the moon
And felt unhappy about staying there.
You jumped off the bright side into darkness
And told me about it on your return.

Morning

poem beginning with a line of Barbara Guest

Morning traverses her breasts'
Shadow-casting nipples:
Her navel brims with darkness
Her thighs will concentrate.

Mirror

poem beginning & ending with a line of Giuseppe Ungaretti

Dear one distant as in a mirror
Having stepped out from bevelled rainbows
And passed where we would be laid to rest
And gone on walking towards the islands
Dear one distant as in a mirror

Snowdrop

Saffron Dilly, silversmith,
Creator of dragonflies
That alight on lapels, leaves
And flowers, has made for you
On your eightieth birthday one
Snowdrop that summarises
Thousands brightening a field,
Three petals, a silver chain,
A perennial springtime
Dangling where your breasts begin.

Winifred's Flowers

after Winifred Nicholson: a found poem

My paintbrush always gives
A tremor of pleasure when
I let it paint a flower—and I
Think I know why this is so—
Flowers mean different things
To different people—to some
They are trophies to decorate
Their dwellings (for this plastic
Flowers will do as well as
Real ones)—to some they are
Buttonholes for their conceit—
To botanists they are species
And tabulated categories—
To bees of course they are
Honey—to me they are the
Secret of the cosmos.

Bog Asphodel

I hope I'm growing old the way bog asphodel
Grows old, seed capsules in October lovely as
The summer flower-spike's radiance, or nearly,
Rusty-orange beacons of the underground.

Bog Cotton

old age
of the wind

landscape
growing old

White Helleborine

after Sarah Raven

Looking for white heliotrope (see Arthur
Symons' poem rhyming 'if' and 'handkerchief')
I find in Sarah Raven's florilegium
White helleborine, in dappled shade
A ghostly flower, a sea shell that never
Fully opens, self-pollinating, self-
Absorbed, a neatly turned-out spinster,
A plant that lives a very private life.

Solomon's-Seal

Shaded by the self-seeded hazels
In a back corner of our garden,
To the right of the flowering currant
An unexpected Solomon's-seal
I want to show you. Does it matter
Why such graceful bells are so called
(Seals of a medieval document?)
It's May, and Solomon says: *Rise up,*
My love, my fair one, and come away,
Winter is past, the rain is over
And gone, flowers appear on the earth.
A solitary cowslip has survived
Under our beech the first grass-cutting.
The time of the singing of birds is come.

Tree

Didn't we choose our home,
Dear, all those years ago
Because of the beech tree,
Beech mast and leaf litter,
Entangled constellations
And the sound of the wind,
Mossy roots for childhood,
For sick and dying friends
A weeping canopy?

Dream

I dreamed I had written a poem
About the beech tree in our garden.
I tried to find it in my notebook.
I sensed the beech tree taking shape,
Three hundred years of summer leaves.

Needlework

for Daphne Tyrrell

Inspired by Mary McDiarmid
Your artistic grandmother, you
Pick up your embroidery hoop
And complete after many years
Flowers you started as a girl,
Recalling her and who you were
In a needlework sunburst:
The flowers are everlasting.

Flowers

poem ending with a line of Christopher Smart

Let us gather sea asters for his ankle and wrist
For flowers are peculiarly the poetry of Christ.

Embroidery

Can you imagine Mary McDiarmid
Selecting silks from her work-basket
And embroidering for you by lamplight
Tablecloths, napkins, dressing-table
Sets, cushion covers, dolls' dresses
With her own designs—marigolds,
Roses, hollyhocks, lupins, violets,
Michaelmas daisies—flowers and buds
In abstract herbaceous borders,
Stem stitch, satin stitch, feather stitch,
Stitches that never come undone,
And for their protection over time
Gathering up within the hoop
All her great-great-grandchildren.

Tapestry

She kept them at bay, those ithyphallic suitors,
Their marriage proposals, sexual advances.

She asked for time to finish her web of deceit,
Unravelling each day's handiwork by torchlight.

Because of the scenes and characters she undid
Penelope's tapestry was a masterpiece.

Penelope's Birds

Her mood-swings remind her of the nightingale's
Complicated spring-time variations;
In a nightmare about her beloved geese
Being slaughtered she sees her suitors killed;
There's a benevolent eagle overhead;
Ornithological Penelope persists:
On how to escape sexual harassment
And bullying she has sought advice from
An eagle, homely geese, a nightingale.

Swifts

The goddess slipped her tongue between my lips—
'Let us run away together,' she said.
We got no farther than the fire-escape,

And from there we watched the swifts ascending
To clouds and sleep and mating on the wing
Oh, how they screeched after each cloacal kiss!

Feast

I

He lined up a sharp-pointed arrow for Antinoös
Who was about to raise a splendid two-handled
Golden drinking cup, balance it, and take a sip,
Bloodshed the last thing on his mind (who'd have thought
A single man among so many at their feast,
However strong, would risk evil death and black fate?).

II

Odysseus took aim and struck him in the gullet,
The barbed arrow-head severing tender sinews.
Antinoös slumped and let fall the golden cup.
A thick jet of life-blood gushed from his nostrils and
(A reflex spasm) he kicked the table over,
Food everywhere, bread and roast meat ruined by gore.

III

The suitors stampeded shit-scared through the hall
Like cattle in springtime driven demented
By horse-flies. Like falcons with hooked talons
Swooping down from the hills to kill passerines
Odysseus and his accomplices rampaged
Cracking skulls until the floor foamed with blood.

Father & Son

When he felt certain who his father was
Telemachos tightly hugged Odysseus—
After twenty years apart and overcome
By a deep longing for lamentation, both
Wailed as ear-piercingly as sea eagles
Whose unfledged nestlings farmers snatch
From the eyrie—such grief-laden tears
Raining down from under their eyelids
(Because I love my own son, I omit
From this simile vultures and their claws)
The sun would have set on their weeping.

Telemachos

Daniel my son, my Telemachos,
Funnier than I am, far cleverer,
Crossword virtuoso, scrabble champ,
Professor of molecular biology
Waging war in your laboratory against
The ghastly crab, and with chemicals
Hoodwinking tumours to devour themselves
(Would Hermes' gift of moly be any use,
That antidote for Circe's sorcery—
Only an onion some scholars think—so
How about poetry's abracadabra
Which gives everything a second chance?)
You wait for my return to Ithaca,
You keep me going on this odyssey.

Cassandra

Which songbird would I choose to represent
Cassandra—our own blackbird, or the nightingale
That gale-force winds have buffeted to Ireland
Or, lost in its vast aria, the wren, or the chiffchaff,
Or the redbreast foretelling the end of the world
In its autumn lament? Who will believe her song
When she faces the cameras and microphones?
The dawn chorus is broadcasting fake news.

Flycatcher

A flycatcher crashed against the window.
Amelia cradled the corpse in her hands
And tried to breathe life into breast-speckles,
Imagining a mossy clearing where
Shadowy trees intertwine, branches
From which to loop and glide and, arrow-
Swift, chase butterflies and stinging bees,
A fledgling like herself, wing-flurry
Flashing in the sun, a little bird
Practising its name and trajectory.

Eagle

Silent ascension
Above Angel Hill,
Conveyor of souls,

And then the remains
In rusty bracken,
Lamb's leg, otter's tail.

Ravens

The first time I go out
The Dooaghtry ravens
Just happen to be there
In the sky, the cottage
To them a huge boulder
Into which we vanish,
Out of which we are born:
Sitting alone you hear
The ravens anticipate
The last time I'll go in.

Swallows

for Ethna Viney

Have the swallows returned,
Ethna, to your woodshed,
Their Thallabaun address,
Your household's annex?

Your hospitality
Every year makes room
For Saharan travellers
And for me from Belfast.

I sit at your table
While swallows feed their young
Penetrating darkness
Through the narrowest gap.

You who are ninety now
Have the swallow's genius
To find above a door
Soul-space, an inch of it.

House Martins

God-sparks metallic blue
With white pantaloons, dawn
Silhouettes, dream birds
At Stone-in-Oxney, then
Cardoso, a composer's
Musical notation
On telegraph wires, higher
Than swallows soaring,
Lower than swifts, their eggs
Precarious pearls
In adhesive bowls, mud
In their mouths, house martins.

Nightingale

in memory of June Newson

You took Fleur Adcock and me to hear
A nightingale near Stone-in-Oxney.
Why didn't June come with us, your good wife
So adept at picking out life's melodies?

I remember for June, wherever she is,
What many years ago that nightingale
Improvised among the trees and shadows:
Cheer-up-cheer-up-woo-it-woo-it-troo-troo-troo

Operator

Ruth Fainlight communicates love
In quietude to Alan Sillitoe,
Her celestial radio-operator
Who brought from Malaya his brassy key,

While she who counts with fingertips
And under her breath the stresses,
Learns from the pattern of syllable
And silence the soul's Morse code.

Poem

Every syllable—
Shh!—has to go on
Reverberating
As though your mouth
Were a Tibetan
Singing bowl.

Sappho

for Gail McConnell

I

How much of what we scribble down survives—
Sappho's miraculous bits and pieces,
Dialect words for kitchen-utensils,
See-through dresses, moonbeams—somebody
At a busy street corner advising
Where to shop for chickpeas and mascara.

II

Let blank spaces between parentheses
Be annotated thus by me and you
Who loiter in the margin, Sapphic souls—
Silence that has lasted a thousand years
Is poetry of a kind, Gail, poetry
Like a brain-child impatient to be born

III

O suburban parthenogenesis,
I eavesdrop on a holy family—
Sappho would have fallen for Beth and you—
Two mothers, two wives, a baby boy's
Thumb-sucking bliss, glistening eyelids,
Hazel-nuts safe beneath a Lesbos sky.

Goldfinch

This drawing of a goldfinch
Is signed by you, Amelia,
Nature note and emblem,
Red face, yellow wing-bars
Its kenspeckles, beak open
For the thistle-bird's song:
At seven you capture all
The finches I'll ever know.

Ornithology

Her feathery drawing
Takes less than a minute:
A dumpy little bird
Has crossed the Sahara.

Wren

Parkinson's Disease makes Paul
Draw and paint very slowly—
This wren portrait, for instance,
The hedgerow polygamist
With his bramble aria
And exquisite wing-coverts
And creamy supercilium
Lingering for many hours
Before—look!—disappearing
Into his hidey-hole.

Dragonfly

Maisie cups in her hands all the way home
A dragonfly, then through the magnifying
Glass I gave you at her age you depict
Wings as though they are cathedral windows
And bring back to life for the family
The insect and its shadow, dear daughter.

Agony

after Giuseppe Ungaretti

To die like the skylark
parched on a mirage

Or like a tired quail
after crossing the sea
losing the will to fly and
dying in the first bushes

But not to live lamenting
like a blinded goldfinch

Helen's Starlings

Helen has conjured starlings from brake shoes,
Ball bearings for eyes, shelf brackets for tails,
The legs old nails, new nails the toes, wings
Plough mower blades, the feathers scissors,
Knives, fork handles, ornithological scrap,
A metallic murmuration on a fence.

Two Bulls

Let me introduce your Clashnettie bull
To my Kildalkey bull—Elvis, Victor—
Yours made of iron and air, mine of flesh and bone,
A sculpture, a poem—the white around the words,
Helen, like the spaces in your metalwork
Through which to contemplate Aberdeenshire
And, in the far distance, a Meath meadow.
Elvis's pizzle demands a wishbone
(Multi-link rear suspension), his scrotum
A motorbike petrol tank (British). Listen
As Victor lends Elvis his Homeric roar.

Primate

Rungwecebus kipunji

Think of being discovered
Among forest shadows,
Leafy lianas that fit
Your fingers and toes,
Over your shoulders
A silvery kimono,
Your soul awaiting
The echo of your name.

Bikini Atoll

A turtle into famine steers,
On her slow shoulders heaves
The burning hinterland,
Her ancient face hung with tears.

Toad

Maisie and Amelia are taking turns
To hold the common warty olive-green
Toad they discovered on their Ard Hill walk.

When Peter my dead twin and I were boys
We were slow to pick up vulnerable frogs,
Worried our hands might scald their undersides.

Granddaughters, toad-entertaining princesses,
Gently in a puddle set the creature down.

Scrimshaw

The tooth of a sperm whale,
A walrus or narwhal tusk,
Space enough for scrimshaw—
His sweetheart's portrait
Scratched by a mariner
In the smelly fo'c'sle
Onto the loneliness
Of an oceanic voyage
Through bloodstained waters.

Origami

Why shouldn't they make use of my failures,
Early versions, outlines, my granddaughters
Conjuring frogs and birds out of scrap paper
And laying my lost words on a swan's wing?

Web

My granddaughters unravel a rainbow
And, weaving a web from the coloured strings,
Incorporating ultraviolet, infrared,
Hang up their web to trap a big idea.

Takabuti

in the Ulster Museum

My granddaughters stare down at her,
A petite fashion-conscious Egyptian
Not much older than they are, her face
Darkened by incense and time, her linen
Eyeballs returning their gaze, her hand
By her side as though to welcome them,
Her foot poking out of the bandages
As though to follow them to the exit
And accompany the rest of their lives.

Beech Bowls

Roger Bennett, woodturner,
Has turned into four bowls
Storm-damage, the long arm
Gale and old age removed
From our mighty beech, bowls
With inky contour-lines
And spalting scribbles for
Great-grandchildren to hold
As though at a picnic
Underneath the canopy.

Teapot

In a Gwen John painting the mantelpiece
Is uncluttered as a rule: on the table
No more than cup and saucer and milk jug,
A brown teapot she makes transcendental.

Sister

for Catherine Longley

You wed my twin and became my sister,
Womb-shadow, playmate, from the ash tree
Dropping into the field behind our house,

Racing beside us on our Hercules bikes
Down the stony road to the Minnowburn
And the Giant's Ring like a radar dish.

We three held hands when he was dying,
A child's game, in our crabapple tree-house
Sharing the silence with a blackbird's nest.

Four Hearts

You were playing bridge on the day you died,
Catherine, my twin's widow, sister-in-law.
So, did you win or lose bidding four hearts?
I was listening to Mussorgsky's death songs
When I heard, and through the kitchen window
Watching a wren near the watering can
Search the brickwork of our home for spiders
And, balanced on suet-filled coconut shells,
Little birds putting on weight for winter.
Bird-gossip was part of our friendliness
As well as fags and gin 'n' tonic mischief
(Until I gave up both, 'traitor to the cause'
You joked, though in your way half serious).
Six long-tailed tits keep coming and going.

Bouquet

Your whisper on the phone
I cannot understand
Though I pretend I can.
Soon I shall send a wreath.

These words in the meantime
Are just a wee bouquet:
Rain-bent autumn crocus,
Honeysuckle tendrils.

Funeral

The day Catherine died
Sarah found a dead wren
Outside her studio:
She lifted it up
On a teaspoon and
Carried it with care
To its bracken grave.

Ashes

They arrive in a little box,
My twin Peter and his widow
Quarantined outside in the porch
Until I bring into the warmth
Their mingled ashes, a portion,
The rest afloat on the North Sea.

I shall drive them to Drumbo Church
And lay them in our parents' grave
With its view across the valley
To Belfast Lough and the shipyard
Where my twin was an apprentice,
The marine engineer to be.

In the shadow of the round tower
I shall be his best man again.

Amateur

In his last years my dad took up painting,
Imagined landscapes to begin with—yachts
That snuggled in their harbour, overwhelmed
By a huge geranium in the foreground—
'I want to grab hold of the stem,' I said.
We hung it cheaply framed above the piano.
Then, a re-arranged Donegal—haystacks
Where they were needed, a red wheelbarrow,
A yellowish towpath going nowhere.
Prognathous, chain-smoking, an amateur
Leaning into perpetual summertime,
Squeezing rainbows onto a dinner plate,
My dad painted to please himself and me,
For eternity a weekend painter—
'Should I move Muckish a little to the left?'

Duets

Happiness is watching my mother and sister
Making room for each other on the piano stool
And playing Schubert duets—laughter, wrong notes—
The melodies surviving—at the french window
My father smiling in—breast-pocket hankie
And cravat even when gardening—his grey hair
Breeze-lifted—beside me on the sofa Peter
My twin amazed as I am by the music-making—
'Don't stop!' Our mother plays us 'Rustle of Spring'.

Seascape

You followed our father towards the end
And painted this picture of the ocean,
A mariner's desolate horizontal.
Is it up to me, Peter, to name the hue—
Lapis lazuli, spring gentian, larkspur
Or sapphire (our mother's engagement ring)?
I want to call the white streak spindrift.
The yellow horizon could be dawn or dusk.
Our father and you are dead, a soldier,
A sailor, the three of us amateurs
Looking out to sea for inspiration
And making it up as we go along.

Shell

The spring tide keeps us from walking any farther
Towards the sea, so we sit on a reedy bank
And you pick out from wool and seaweed and droppings
A shell and slip into your handbag its spirals
With the fisherman's float I rescued from the lake
Where, more than fifty years ago, we honeymooned.
The ravens in conversation overhead might be
Discussing us or that sheep dead in a hollow
With its yellow ear-tag and delicate black feet.

Wreck

Neighbours have pulled asunder my ship of death
—The old wreck with its cargo of sandy water—
Tractors and ropes and chains on Thallabaun strand,
Spars hard as stone dismembered for gate-posts
And barn-lintels. Where are the tree-pegs now
That held together my oblivion-boat
At the edge of the surf among sanderlings?
At spring tide where will my soul be going?

Seahorses

Did I write about myself
In a discarded lyric
That rises to the surface:
The eggs are incubated
By the male of the species,
Heraldic the horse's head
Though his body convulses
Pumping into the sea sons
And daughters—his stomach's
Hundred tiny versions—
Their death a dignified drift
And a slow coming to light
On the shore? Seahorses.
Am I repeating myself?

Totem

When the tree-surgeon cut away
From our top-heavy beech a ton,
I assembled in my mind's eye logs
As a star-surrounded totem pole
With carvings of all the creatures—
Concussed tawny owl, sleepy
Pot-bellied badger, otter drowned
In the eel-trap, Rosemary's donkeys,
Emma's punctual frogs, hares
And stoats playing scary games
Around the erratic boulder—O all
In a ghost dance with my twin brother
And the dead poets and my warrior
Father and my mother with her limp.

Turlough

Inspiration is the water
In a turlough that comes and goes,
An unfathomable swallow-hole:
Fen violet's water-colours,
A damselfly spreading its wings.

Wet Stars

I have stirred up—beyond the stepping stones
At spring tide—imagination—just look—
Momentary constellations—wet stars
Underfoot—phosphorescence—waterburn—

Acknowledgements

I shall forever be indebted to David Cabot, great ornitho-logist and dear friend, for the priceless gift of time spent at Carrigskeewaun. I have journeyed there every year since 1970. David Cabot is the godfather of more than half of my lifetime's poems.

In the course of writing *The Slain Birds* I have been inspired by the generous support of Mark Pigott KBE, poetry's friend and champion. I also thank Sarah Longley for her exquisite cover drawing of a dead goldcrest. It has been a privilege to explore Homer's world in the company of the distinguished Greek scholar Maureen Alden. The first readers of these poems have been Edna Longley, Fran Brearton, Frank Ormsby, and Patricia Craig. I thank them for their continuing patience and perspicacity.

Notes

In 'Dartford Warbler' Jeff is the painter Jeffrey Morgan; Edward is Edward Thomas. In 'Nightingale' I add just one syllable to John Clare's transliteration of the nightingale's song.

'Dear Mother' versifies Private Herbert Beattie's letter home from the trenches of the Great War. I found this devastating document in *Ulster and the First World War* by Jonathan Bardon (Northern Ireland War Memorial): the letter was transcribed for him by Kathleen Page.

I found 'Maps of Gloucestershire' in *Under Storm's Wing* by Helen Thomas (Carcanet Press); 'Winifred's Flowers' in the Kettle's Yard publication *Winifred Nicholson: Music of Colour*. In 'White Helleborine' I borrow phrases from Sarah Raven's marvellous florilegium *Wild Flowers* (Bloomsbury). For 'Mirror' and 'Agony' I have turned to Patrick Creagh's indispensable translation of Giuseppe Ungaretti's *Selected Poems* (Penguin).

'Embroidery' was written for *Days of Clear Light*, a Festschrift in honour of Jessie Lendennie (Salmon Poetry); 'Operator' for *For Ruth*, a celebration of Ruth Fainlight at ninety (CB Editions).

'Cassandra' and 'Penelope's Birds' were included in *Homer's Octopus*, a chapbook of my Homer-inspired poems (with drawings by Sarah Longley), published in 2020 by Andrew Moorhouse of Fine Press Poetry.

Early versions of 'Seahorses' and 'Bikini Atoll' appeared in *Lares*, a pamphlet published in 1972 by Alan Tarling's Poet & Printer Press, and illustrated by Brian Ferran. Helen Denerley creates her magical sculptures (made out of scrap metal) at Clashnettie in Aberdeenshire.

Some words may require a gloss: *smudging*: a purifying ceremony; *townland*: a rural term for an area of land that varies from a few acres to thousands; *dander*: stroll, saunter; *hockerty-cockerty*: 'seated with one's legs astride another's shoulders'; *yellow flags*: wild irises; *kenspeckles*: distinguishing features; *spalting*: wood colouration caused by fungi; *turloughs*: 'transient lakes that occur in hollows and appear when the water table breaks the surface and the water appears above ground' (Cabot & Goodwillie, *The Burren*, William Collins).

Some of these poems have appeared previously in *Agenda, Archipelago, The Dark Horse, The Guardian, Irish Pages, The Irish Times, The London Review of Books, The New Yorker, Poetry Ireland Review, The Robert Graves Review*; and on RTÉ and BBC.

my grandson
and namesake
says the dark
is where you
can see what
you're thinking